BUILDING BLOCKS OF PROGRAMMING LANGUAGES

COMPILERS AND INTERPRETERS

OLIVER LUCAS JR

Copyright © 2024 by Oliver Lucas Jr

All rights reserved. No part of this publication may be reproduced, distributed, or transmitted in any form or by any means, including photocopying, recording, or other electronic or mechanical methods, without the prior written permission of the publisher, except in the case of brief quotations embodied in critical reviews and certain other non commercial uses permitted by copyright law.

TABLE OF CONTENTS

Chapter 1

1.1 What is a Programming Language?
1.2 The Role of Compilers and Interpreters
1.3 Types of Programming Languages

Chapter 2

2.1 Regular Expressions and Finite Automata
2.2 Lexical Analyzer Design
2.3 Tokenization and Symbol Table

Chapter 3

3.1 Context-Free Grammars and Parsing Trees
3.2 Top-Down Parsing: Recursive Descent and Predictive Parsing
3.3 Bottom-Up Parsing: Shift-Reduce and LR Parsing

Chapter 4

4.1 Static Semantic Analysis: Type Checking and Scope Resolution
4.2 Dynamic Semantic Analysis: Runtime Type Checking and Error Handling
4.3 Intermediate Code Generation

Chapter 5

5.1 Three-Address Code
5.2 Static Single Assignment Form
5.3 Control Flow Graphs (CFGs)

Chapter 6

6.1 High-Level Optimizations
6.2 Low-Level Optimizations: Register Allocation and Instruction Scheduling

Chapter 7

7.1 Target Machine Architecture
7.2 Instruction Selection and Code Emission
7.3 Code Optimization for Specific Architectures

Chapter 8

8.1 Memory Management: Stack, Heap, and Garbage Collection
8.2 Exception Handling
8.3 Input/Output Operations

Chapter 9

9.1 Virtual Machines and Bytecode
9.2 Interpreter Design and Implementation
9.3 Just-In-Time Compilation

Chapter 10

10.1 Domain-Specific Languages (DSLs)
10.2 Compiler Construction Tools
10.3 Parallel and Distributed Compilation

Preface
Unveiling the Architecture of Programming Languages

In the intricate tapestry of modern computing, programming languages serve as the essential tools that empower us to craft digital solutions. Yet, beneath the surface of these languages lies a complex architecture, a carefully designed framework that enables us to communicate with machines in a structured and efficient manner.

This book delves into the core concepts and principles that underpin programming language design and implementation. We embark on a journey through the labyrinthine world of compilers, interpreters, and virtual machines, exploring the fundamental building blocks that shape the way we write and execute code.

Within these pages, you will discover:

The evolution of programming languages: From early assembly languages to modern, high-level languages.

The art of language design: The key considerations and trade-offs involved in designing programming languages.

The magic of compilers: How compilers translate human-readable code into machine code.

The versatility of interpreters: The role of interpreters in executing code dynamically.

The power of virtual machines: How virtual machines provide a platform-independent execution environment.

The nuances of memory management: The techniques used to efficiently allocate and deallocate memory.

The elegance of exception handling: How to gracefully handle errors and exceptions.

The intricacies of I/O operations: The mechanisms for interacting with the outside world.

The optimization of code: Strategies for improving the performance of programs.

The future of programming languages: Emerging trends and cutting-edge technologies.

This book is intended for anyone who is curious about the inner workings of programming languages, from students and hobbyists to experienced programmers and compiler developers. Whether you're looking to deepen your understanding of language design, improve your programming skills, or simply satisfy your intellectual curiosity, this book will provide you with a comprehensive and insightful exploration.

Let us embark on this intellectual adventure together.

Chapter 1

Introduction to Programming Languages and Translation

1.1 What is a Programming Language?

A programming language is a set of instructions that humans can use to communicate with computers. These instructions are written in a specific syntax and grammar, which the computer can understand and interpret.

Think of it like a human language. We use words and grammar to communicate with each other, and computers use programming languages to understand and execute tasks.

Here are some key points about programming languages:

Syntax: The rules and structure of a language.

Semantics: The meaning of the language's constructs.

High-level vs. Low-level: High-level languages are closer to human language, while low-level languages are closer to machine code.

Paradigms: Different approaches to programming, such as procedural, object-oriented, and functional.

By learning a programming language, you can create software, automate tasks, and solve complex problems.

1.2 The Role of Compilers and Interpreters

Compilers and interpreters are essential tools that bridge the gap between human-readable programming languages and machine code, which computers can directly understand.

Compilers

A **compiler** translates the entire source code of a program into machine code in one go. This process involves several stages:

1 **Lexical Analysis:** Breaking down the code into tokens (keywords, identifiers, operators, etc.).

2 **Syntax Analysis:** Checking the grammatical structure of the code.

3 **Semantic Analysis:** Analyzing the meaning of the code.

4 **Intermediate Code Generation:** Creating an intermediate representation of the code.

5 **Code Optimization:** Improving the efficiency of the code.

6 **Code Generation:** Translating the optimized code into machine code.

Once compiled, the program can be executed directly by the computer without the need for further translation. This results in faster execution times, as the translation process is done only once.

Interpreters

An **interpreter** translates and executes the code line by line. It doesn't create a separate executable file. Instead, it reads each line of code, translates it into machine code, and executes it immediately.

This approach offers more flexibility, as changes to the code can be made and tested immediately. However, it can be slower than compiled programs, as the translation process happens at runtime.

Key Differences:

Feature	Compiler	Interpreter
Translation Process	Once, before execution	Line by line, during execution
Output	Executable file	No executable file
Execution Speed	Faster	Slower
Debugging	More difficult	Easier
Flexibility	Less flexible	More flexible

Common Use Cases:

Compilers: Used for system software, game engines, and other performance-critical applications.

Interpreters: Used for scripting languages, web development, and rapid prototyping.

In some cases, a hybrid approach is used, where a compiler translates the code into an intermediate form (like bytecode), which is then interpreted by a virtual machine. This approach offers a balance between performance and flexibility.

1.3 Types of Programming Languages

Programming languages can be categorized based on their programming paradigm or purpose. Here are some of the most common types:

1. Procedural Programming Languages

Focus: Breaking down a problem into a sequence of steps.

Examples: C, Pascal, Fortran

Characteristics: Uses procedures or functions to organize code.

2. Object-Oriented Programming Languages

Focus: Modeling real-world entities as objects with properties and behaviors.

Examples: Java, C++, Python, C#

Characteristics: Uses concepts like classes, objects, inheritance, and polymorphism.

3. Functional Programming Languages

Focus: Treating computation as the evaluation of mathematical functions.

Examples: Haskell, Lisp, Erlang

Characteristics: Emphasizes pure functions, immutability, and recursion.

4. Scripting Languages

Focus: Automating tasks and creating scripts.

Examples: Python, JavaScript, Ruby, Perl

Characteristics: Often interpreted, have a simpler syntax, and are used for rapid development.

5. Logic Programming Languages

Focus: Declarative programming, where the programmer specifies what needs to be computed rather than how.

Examples: Prolog

Characteristics: Uses logical rules and inference to solve problems.

6. Domain-Specific Languages (DSLs)

Focus: Designed for a specific domain or problem.

Examples: SQL (for databases), HTML/CSS (for web development), LaTeX (for document formatting)

Characteristics: Often embedded within a general-purpose language or have their own interpreters.

7. Low-Level Languages

Focus: Directly interacting with hardware.

Examples: Assembly language, machine code

Characteristics: Difficult to learn and use, but offer high performance and control over hardware.

8. High-Level Languages

Focus: Easier to read and write, closer to human language.

Examples: Python, Java, C#

Characteristics: Abstract away low-level details, making programming more accessible.

The choice of programming language depends on various factors, including the specific task, performance requirements, developer preferences, and the availability of libraries and tools.

Chapter 2

Lexical Analysis

2.1 Regular Expressions and Finite Automata

Regular expressions and finite automata are fundamental concepts in computer science, particularly in the realm of text processing and pattern matching. They are closely related, with finite automata providing a formal mathematical model for representing regular expressions.

Regular Expressions

A regular expression is a sequence of characters that defines a search pattern. They are used to match specific patterns within text strings.

Basic Regular Expression Syntax:

Literal characters: Match themselves.

Metacharacters: Special characters with specific meanings.

. : Matches any single character.

* : Matches zero or more occurrences of the preceding element.

+ : Matches one or more occurrences of the preceding element.

? : Matches zero or one occurrence of the preceding element.

[ ]: Matches a character within the specified set.

[^]: Matches a character not within the specified set.

\: Escapes special characters.

Example: To match a phone number in the format "(123) 456-7890", we can use the regular expression: `\(\d{3}\)\s\d{3}-\d{4}`

Finite Automata

A finite automaton is a mathematical model that recognizes a set of strings. It consists of a finite set of states and a set of transitions between states.

Types of Finite Automata:

1 Deterministic Finite Automaton (DFA):

For each state and input symbol, there is exactly one transition.

Efficient for pattern matching.

2 Non-deterministic Finite Automaton (NFA):

For a given state and input symbol, there can be multiple transitions.

More expressive than DFAs but less efficient.

Relationship Between Regular Expressions and Finite Automata:

Regular expressions can be converted into equivalent finite automata.

Finite automata can be used to implement regular expression matching algorithms.

Applications:

Text Search: Finding specific patterns in text documents.

Input Validation: Validating user input to ensure it conforms to specific patterns.

Network Protocols: Parsing and processing network protocols.

Lexical Analysis: Breaking down source code into tokens.

By understanding regular expressions and finite automata, you can effectively work with text processing tasks and build robust software applications.

2.2 Lexical Analyzer Design

A lexical analyzer, also known as a lexer or scanner, is a fundamental component of a compiler or interpreter. It breaks down the input source code into meaningful tokens, such as keywords, identifiers, operators, and literals.

Key Components of a Lexical Analyzer:

1 Input Buffer: Stores the input source code.

2 Finite Automata: Recognizes patterns in the input stream.

3 Token Table: Stores information about recognized tokens, including their type and value.

Design Steps:

1 Define the Token Set:

Identify the set of tokens that the language recognizes.

For example: keywords, identifiers, operators, numbers, strings, etc.

2 Design the Finite Automata:

Create a finite automaton to recognize each token type.

The automaton can be deterministic or non-deterministic, depending on the complexity of the language.

3 Implement the Lexical Analyzer:

Read the input character by character.

Use the finite automaton to match the input against token patterns.

When a token is recognized, create a token object and store it in the token table.

If no token is recognized, report an error.

Example:

Consider a simple language with keywords `if`, `else`, `while`, identifiers, integers, and operators +, -, *, /.

The finite automaton for recognizing identifiers might look like this:

```
Start -> Letter -> (Letter | Digit)*
```

Where:

`Start` is the initial state.

`Letter` represents any letter.

`Digit` represents any digit.

The lexical analyzer would read the input character by character and try to match it against the defined patterns. If a match is found, it would create a token object with the token type "identifier" and the token value (the actual identifier string).

Challenges in Lexical Analyzer Design:

Handling Keywords: Distinguishing between keywords and identifiers.

Recognizing Numbers: Handling different number formats (integer, floating-point).

Handling Comments: Ignoring comments and whitespace.

Error Handling: Reporting meaningful error messages for invalid input.

By carefully designing and implementing the lexical analyzer, we can ensure the correct parsing and semantic analysis of the source code.

2.3 Tokenization and Symbol Table

Tokenization

Tokenization is the process of breaking down a sequence of characters (source code) into meaningful units called tokens. These tokens are the building blocks for further analysis by the compiler or interpreter.

Key Steps in Tokenization:

1 Read Input: The lexical analyzer reads the input character by character.

2 Identify Lexemes: The lexer identifies sequences of characters that form lexemes (the actual text of a token).

3 Classify Tokens: Each lexeme is classified into a specific token type (e.g., keyword, identifier, operator, literal).

4 Create Tokens: A token object is created for each recognized token, containing its type and value.

Example: For the code `int x = 10;`, the tokenizer would break it down into the following tokens:

`KEYWORD`: `int`

`IDENTIFIER`: `x`

`OPERATOR`: `=`

`INTEGER_LITERAL`: `10`

`SEMICOLON`: `;`

Symbol Table

A symbol table is a data structure used to store information about identifiers, such as their type, scope, and value. It is crucial for semantic analysis and code generation.

Key Elements of a Symbol Table:

Identifier: The name of the variable, function, or other entity.

Type: The data type of the identifier (e.g., integer, float, string).

Scope: The region of the program where the identifier is valid.

Value: The current value of the identifier (if applicable).

Attributes: Other relevant information, such as memory address, function parameters, etc.

Symbol Table Operations:

Insertion: Adding a new entry to the symbol table.

Lookup: Searching for an existing entry in the symbol table.

Deletion: Removing an entry from the symbol table when it goes out of scope.

Example: For the code `int x = 10;`, the symbol table might contain the following entry:

Identifier	Type	Scope	Value
x	int	global	10

By using a symbol table, the compiler or interpreter can keep track of variables, functions, and other entities, ensuring that they are used correctly and consistently throughout the program.

Chapter 3

Syntax Analysis

3.1 Context-Free Grammars and Parsing Trees

Context-Free Grammars (CFGs)

A Context-Free Grammar (CFG) is a formal grammar that defines a formal language. It consists of a set of production rules, each rule specifying a non-terminal symbol and its possible expansions.

Example:

```
S -> NP VP
NP -> Det N | NP PP
VP -> V NP | VP PP
PP -> P NP
Det -> the | a
N -> cat | dog | book
V -> saw | liked
P -> with | on
```

In this grammar:

S is the start symbol.

Non-terminal symbols are enclosed in angle brackets (< >).

Terminal symbols are words like "the," "cat," "saw," etc.

A derivation is a sequence of applications of production rules to derive a string of terminal symbols from the start symbol.

19

Parsing Trees

A parsing tree is a graphical representation of a derivation. It shows how a string of terminal symbols can be derived from the start symbol using the production rules of a CFG.

Example: For the string "the cat saw a dog with a book," a possible parsing tree could be:

```
         S
        / \
      NP   VP
     / \   | \
   Det  N  V  NP
   /    \  |  | \
 the    cat saw Det N  PP
                 |   | \
                 a  dog P  NP
                        |  | \
                       with Det N
                             | \
                            the book
```

Types of Parsing:

1 Top-Down Parsing:

Recursive Descent Parsing: A top-down parsing technique that directly implements the grammar's production rules.

Predictive Parsing: A top-down parsing technique that uses a lookahead symbol to determine the next production rule to apply.

2 Bottom-Up Parsing:

Shift-Reduce Parsing: A bottom-up parsing technique that involves shifting input symbols onto a stack and reducing them to non-terminal symbols using production rules.

LR Parsing: A powerful bottom-up parsing technique that uses a parsing table to guide the parsing process.

Parsing techniques are essential for compilers and interpreters to analyze the syntactic structure of source code and generate appropriate semantic representations.

3.2 Top-Down Parsing: Recursive Descent and Predictive Parsing

Top-down parsing is a parsing technique that starts from the start symbol of a grammar and progressively derives the input string by applying production rules. Two common top-down parsing techniques are:

Recursive Descent Parsing

Recursive descent parsing is a straightforward approach where each non-terminal in the grammar is represented by a recursive procedure. The parser starts with the start symbol and recursively calls procedures for non-terminals, matching the input tokens against the production rules.

Key Points:

Simple implementation: It's relatively easy to implement, especially for simple grammars.

Backtracking: It may require backtracking if a wrong production rule is chosen, which can be inefficient for complex grammars.

Left recursion: It can handle left-recursive grammars, but often requires additional techniques to avoid infinite recursion.

Predictive Parsing

Predictive parsing is a more efficient variant of recursive descent parsing that avoids backtracking. It uses a lookahead token to determine the appropriate production rule to apply at each step.

Key Points:

No backtracking: It eliminates the need for backtracking, making it more efficient.

LL(1) grammars: It requires LL(1) grammars, which have the property that the next production rule can be determined by looking at the current non-terminal and the next input token.

Parsing table: It often uses a parsing table to guide the parsing process, making it more efficient.

Example:

Consider the following grammar:

```
S -> NP VP
NP -> Det N | NP PP
VP -> V NP | VP PP
Det -> the | a
N -> cat | dog | book
V -> saw | liked
P -> with | on
```

A recursive descent parser would recursively call procedures for `S`, `NP`, `VP`, `Det`, `N`, `V`, and `P`. A predictive parser, on the other hand, would use a parsing table to determine the next production rule based on the current non-terminal and the lookahead token.

In conclusion, both recursive descent and predictive parsing are top-down parsing techniques that can be used to analyze the syntactic structure of input strings. While recursive descent is simpler to implement, predictive parsing is generally more efficient due to its ability to avoid backtracking.

3.3 Bottom-Up Parsing: Shift-Reduce and LR Parsing

Bottom-up parsing is a parsing technique that starts from the input tokens and gradually builds larger syntactic structures until the entire input is reduced to the start symbol of the grammar.

Shift-Reduce Parsing

Shift-reduce parsing is a simple bottom-up parsing technique that involves two operations:

1 Shift: Shifts the next input token onto the top of the stack.

2 Reduce: Reduces a sequence of symbols on the top of the stack to a non-terminal symbol, using a production rule.

Key Points:

Simple implementation: It's relatively easy to implement.

Efficiency: It can be efficient for simple grammars.

Limitations: It may not be suitable for complex grammars with ambiguous or left-recursive constructs.

LR Parsing

LR parsing is a powerful bottom-up parsing technique that uses a parsing table to guide the parsing process. It's more efficient and flexible than shift-reduce parsing.

Key Points:

LR(0), LR(1), SLR(1), LALR(1), and LR(k): Different LR parsing techniques with varying levels of power and complexity.

Parsing table: It uses a parsing table to determine the next action (shift or reduce) based on the current state and the lookahead token.

Error recovery: It can handle errors gracefully and provide informative error messages.

Example:

Consider the following grammar:

```
S -> NP VP
NP -> Det N | NP PP
VP -> V NP | VP PP
Det -> the | a
N -> cat | dog | book
V -> saw | liked
P -> with | on
```

An LR parser would use a parsing table to guide the parsing process. It would start by shifting the first input token onto the stack. Then, it would repeatedly shift and reduce tokens until the entire input is reduced to the start symbol S.

In conclusion, both shift-reduce and LR parsing are bottom-up parsing techniques that can be used to analyze the syntactic structure of input strings. While shift-reduce parsing is simpler, LR parsing is more powerful and efficient, making it a popular choice for compiler construction.

Chapter 4

Semantic Analysis

4.1 Static Semantic Analysis: Type Checking and Scope Resolution

Static semantic analysis is a crucial phase in the compilation process that ensures the semantic correctness of a program before it's executed. It involves two primary tasks:

Type Checking

Type checking verifies that the types of operands in expressions and the types of arguments passed to functions are compatible with the operations being performed. This helps prevent runtime errors that may arise from type mismatches.

Key Concepts:

Type System: A formal system for classifying expressions and values into different types.

Type Inference: The process of automatically determining the types of expressions without explicit type declarations.

Type Compatibility: Rules that determine when two types can be considered compatible.

Example: In a strongly-typed language like Java, the following code would be flagged as a type error:

```Java
int x = 10;
String y = "hello";
```

```
int z = x + y; // Type mismatch: cannot add int
and String
```

Scope Resolution

Scope resolution determines the meaning of identifiers (variables, functions, etc.) within a program. It involves identifying the declaration of an identifier and ensuring that it's accessible from the point of use.

Key Concepts:

Scope: A region of a program where an identifier is valid.

Scope Rules: Rules that govern how scopes are nested and how identifiers are resolved.

Symbol Table: A data structure used to store information about identifiers, including their type, scope, and other attributes.

Example: In the following C++ code, the variable x declared within the if block is only accessible within that block:

C++

```
if (condition) {
    int x = 10;
}
// x is not accessible here
```

Challenges in Static Semantic Analysis:

Complex Type Systems: Languages like C++ and Haskell have complex type systems with features like templates, polymorphism, and operator overloading, which can make type checking challenging.

Dynamic Languages: Languages like Python and JavaScript have dynamic typing, where types are determined at runtime. Static analysis for these languages is more limited.

Scope Rules: Some languages have intricate scope rules, such as those involving closures and modules, which can make scope resolution complex.

By effectively performing static semantic analysis, compilers can catch many potential errors early in the development process, leading to more reliable and robust software.

4.2 Dynamic Semantic Analysis: Runtime Type Checking and Error Handling

Dynamic semantic analysis is the process of checking the semantic correctness of a program at runtime. This is in contrast to static semantic analysis, which is performed at compile time. Dynamic semantic analysis is often used in languages with dynamic typing, where the types of variables are not known until runtime.

Runtime Type Checking

Runtime type checking involves verifying the types of operands and function arguments at the time of execution. If a type mismatch is detected, an error is raised. This is a key feature of dynamically typed languages like Python and JavaScript.

Example:

Python
```
x = 10
y = "hello"
```

```
z = x + y   # This will raise a TypeError at runtime
```

Error Handling

Error handling is a crucial aspect of dynamic semantic analysis. It involves detecting and handling errors that may occur during program execution. Common error handling mechanisms include:

1 **Exceptions:** Exceptions are used to signal and handle errors that occur during program execution. They can be raised by the runtime system or by the program itself.

2 **Assertions:** Assertions are used to check for conditions that should always be true. If an assertion fails, an error is raised.

3 **Logging:** Logging is used to record information about the program's execution, including errors and warnings.

Example:

Python

```
try:
    x = 10 / 0
except ZeroDivisionError:
    print("Error: Division by zero")
```

Key Differences between Static and Dynamic Semantic Analysis:

Feature	Static Semantic Analysis	Dynamic Semantic Analysis

Timing	Performed at compile time	Performed at runtime
Type Checking	Strict type checking	Flexible type checking
Error Detection	Catches errors early	Catches errors at runtime
Performance	Can improve performance by optimizing code	Can impact performance due to runtime checks

While dynamic semantic analysis offers flexibility, it can lead to runtime errors that could have been caught earlier in the development process. Therefore, a combination of static and dynamic analysis is often used to ensure the correctness and reliability of software.

4.3 Intermediate Code Generation

Intermediate code generation is a crucial step in the compilation process. It involves transforming the source code into a platform-independent intermediate representation. This intermediate representation is simpler than the original source code but more complex than machine code. It serves as a bridge between the source code and the target machine code.

Why use intermediate code?

Platform independence: The intermediate code can be generated for any source language and can be targeted to any machine architecture.

Optimization opportunities: The intermediate code can be optimized before generating the final machine code.

Code generation simplification: The process of generating machine code from the intermediate code is often simpler than generating it directly from the source code.

Common intermediate representations:

Three-Address Code (TAC): A simple intermediate representation that consists of instructions with at most three operands. Each instruction typically has the form: `result = operand1 op operand2`.

Static Single Assignment (SSA) form: A more advanced intermediate representation where each variable is assigned a value only once. This makes it easier to perform various optimizations.

Control Flow Graphs (CFG): A graphical representation of the control flow of a program. It consists of nodes representing basic blocks and edges representing control flow between blocks.

Intermediate code generation process:

1 Syntax analysis: The source code is parsed to construct a parse tree or abstract syntax tree (AST).

2 Semantic analysis: The semantic meaning of the code is analyzed, and type checking is performed.

3 Intermediate code generation: The AST is transformed into an intermediate representation, such as TAC or SSA form.

4 Optimization: The intermediate code is optimized to improve its efficiency.

5 Code generation: The optimized intermediate code is translated into machine code for the target architecture.

Example of three-address code:

```
a = b + c
d = a * 2
```

```
e = d - 1
```

Can be represented in three-address code as:

```
t1 = b + c
a = t1
t2 = a * 2
d = t2
t3 = d - 1
e = t3
```

By using intermediate code, compilers can achieve better performance, code quality, and portability.

Chapter 5

Intermediate Representation

5.1 Three-Address Code

Three-Address Code (TAC) is a simple intermediate representation used in compilers. It consists of instructions with at most three operands, typically in the form:

```
result = operand1 op operand2
```

Each instruction performs a simple operation, such as arithmetic, logical, or assignment. The operands can be variables, constants, or temporary variables.

Key characteristics of TAC:

Simplicity: TAC is a relatively simple representation that is easy to generate and manipulate.

Efficiency: TAC can be efficiently translated into machine code.

Optimization friendly: Many optimizations can be applied to TAC, such as constant folding, dead code elimination, and strength reduction.

Example:

Consider the following C code:

C
```
int x = 10;
int y = 20;
```

```
int z = x + y;
```

The corresponding TAC would be:

```
t1 = 10
x = t1
t2 = 20
y = t2
t3 = x + y
z = t3
```

Here, `t1`, `t2`, and `t3` are temporary variables used to store intermediate results.

Advantages of using TAC:

Platform independence: TAC can be generated for any source language and can be targeted to any machine architecture.

Code optimization: TAC is a suitable representation for applying various optimization techniques.

Code generation simplification: The process of generating machine code from TAC is often simpler than generating it directly from the source code.

Limitations of TAC:

Limited expressiveness: TAC cannot directly represent complex control flow structures like loops and conditional statements.

Inefficient for certain operations: In some cases, TAC can be less efficient than other intermediate representations, such as Static Single Assignment (SSA) form.

While TAC is a simple and effective intermediate representation, it is often used in conjunction with other representations to achieve better performance and optimization.

5.2 Static Single Assignment Form

Static Single Assignment (SSA) form is an intermediate representation (IR) in compiler design where each variable is assigned a value exactly once. This unique property simplifies many compiler optimizations.

Key characteristics of SSA:

Unique assignment: Each variable is assigned a value only once.

Versioning: To achieve unique assignments, variables are often versioned, meaning they are given different names or indices to distinguish between different definitions.

Φ-functions: These functions are used to merge different definitions of a variable at control flow merge points.

Advantages of SSA:

Simplified analysis: Many compiler analyses, such as data flow analysis and constant propagation, become simpler and more efficient in SSA form.

Improved optimization: SSA enables a wide range of optimizations, including:

Constant propagation

Dead code elimination

Strength reduction

Loop optimization

Register allocation

Clearer representation: SSA can make the program's control flow and data dependencies more explicit, aiding in understanding and debugging.

Example:

Consider the following code:

```c
x = 10;
y = 20;
if (condition) {
    x = x + y;
} else {
    x = x - y;
}
z = x * 2;
```

In SSA form, this code would be represented as:

```
x1 = 10;
y1 = 20;
x2 = φ(x1, x3);
z1 = x2 * 2;
```

Here, x2 is a φ-function that merges the two definitions of x from the `if` and `else` branches.

In conclusion, SSA form is a powerful tool for compiler optimization. By ensuring that each variable is assigned only once, it simplifies analysis and enables a wide range of optimizations.

5.3 Control Flow Graphs (CFGs)

A Control Flow Graph (CFG) is a graphical representation of the control flow of a program. It's a directed graph where nodes represent basic blocks and edges represent the flow of control between blocks.

Basic Block: A basic block is a sequence of instructions that executes sequentially without any branches or jumps within it. It starts with a leader instruction (the target of a branch or the first instruction of the function) and ends with a branch instruction or the end of the function.

Nodes and Edges in a CFG:

Nodes: Represent basic blocks.

Edges: Represent the flow of control between basic blocks.

Entry Node: The starting point of the CFG.

Exit Node: The ending point of the CFG.

Example:

Consider the following C code:

```c
if (condition) {
    // Block 1
} else {
    // Block 2
}
// Block 3
```

The corresponding CFG would look like this:

Uses of CFGs in Compiler Design:

Data Flow Analysis: Analyzing the flow of data through the program to identify optimization opportunities.

Code Optimization: Identifying redundant code, dead code, and other inefficiencies.

Code Generation: Generating efficient machine code.

Testing and Debugging: Analyzing the program's control flow to identify potential errors and test cases.

Key Points:

CFGs provide a visual representation of the program's control flow.

They are used in various compiler optimization techniques.

By analyzing the CFG, we can understand the program's behavior and identify potential issues.

By understanding CFGs, compiler designers can create more efficient and reliable compilers.

Chapter 6

Code Optimization

6.1 High-Level Optimizations

High-level optimizations are techniques applied to the intermediate representation of a program to improve its efficiency and performance. These optimizations are typically performed before code generation. Here are three common high-level optimizations:

1. Constant Folding

Constant folding is a technique that involves evaluating constant expressions at compile time. This can significantly reduce the number of computations performed at runtime.

Example:

C

```
int x = 2 * 3 + 5;
```

After constant folding, this expression can be simplified to:

C

```
int x = 11;
```

2. Dead Code Elimination

Dead code elimination involves removing code that is never executed. This can include unused variables, unreachable code, or code that has no effect on the program's output.

Example:

C

```
int x = 10;
// ... (code that doesn't use x)
```

The declaration of `x` can be removed as it is never used.

3. Loop Optimization

Loop optimization focuses on improving the performance of loops, which are often performance bottlenecks in programs. Several techniques can be used to optimize loops:

Loop Invariant Code Motion: Moving code that does not change within a loop to outside the loop.

Loop Unrolling: Replicating the loop body multiple times to reduce loop overhead.

Strength Reduction: Replacing expensive operations (like multiplication) with cheaper ones (like addition).

Induction Variable Elimination: Eliminating redundant computations of loop induction variables.

Example:

C

```
for (int i = 0; i < 10; i++) {
    x = x + 2;
```

}

After loop invariant code motion and strength reduction:

C

```
int temp = 2 * 10;
for (int i = 0; i < 10; i++) {
    x = x + temp;
}
```

By applying these high-level optimizations, compilers can generate more efficient and optimized code, leading to improved program performance.

6.2 Low-Level Optimizations: Register Allocation and Instruction Scheduling

Low-level optimizations are techniques applied to the machine code generated by a compiler to improve its performance. These optimizations focus on the efficient use of hardware resources, such as registers and memory.

1. Register Allocation

Register allocation is the process of assigning machine registers to variables and temporary values in the program. By effectively allocating registers, we can reduce the number of memory accesses, which can significantly improve performance.

Key techniques for register allocation:

Graph coloring: This technique treats registers as colors and variables as nodes in a graph. The goal is to color the graph with the fewest number of colors (registers) such that no two adjacent nodes have the same color.

Live range analysis: This analysis determines the lifetime of a variable, i.e., the interval between its definition and its last use. Register allocation algorithms can prioritize allocating registers to variables with longer live ranges.

2. Instruction Scheduling

Instruction scheduling is the process of reordering instructions to improve the performance of the generated code. The goal is to maximize instruction-level parallelism by identifying and exploiting instruction-level parallelism (ILP) opportunities.

Key techniques for instruction scheduling:

List scheduling: This technique maintains a list of ready instructions and selects the instruction with the highest priority to be scheduled.

Resource constrained scheduling: This technique considers resource constraints, such as the number of functional units and register availability, when scheduling instructions.

Software pipelining: This technique overlaps the execution of multiple iterations of a loop to hide latency and improve instruction-level parallelism.

By applying these low-level optimizations, compilers can generate highly efficient machine code that can take full advantage of the target hardware's capabilities.

Chapter 7

Code Generation

7.1 Target Machine Architecture

The target machine architecture is the specific hardware platform for which the compiler generates machine code. Understanding the target architecture is crucial for efficient code generation and optimization. Key aspects of a target machine architecture include:

Processor Architecture

Instruction Set Architecture (ISA): The set of instructions that a processor can understand and execute.

Register File: The set of registers available for storing data.

Memory Hierarchy: The organization of memory, including caches and main memory.

Pipeline Stages: The stages through which instructions pass during execution.

Memory System

Memory Organization: The way memory is organized, such as byte-addressable or word-addressable.

Memory Access Patterns: The patterns of memory access, which can impact performance.

Cache Hierarchy: The levels of cache memory and their associated properties.

Input/Output System

I/O Devices: The types of input/output devices supported by the architecture.

I/O Instructions: The instructions used to communicate with I/O devices.

Compiler Considerations for Target Machine Architecture

Instruction Selection: Choosing the appropriate instructions from the ISA to implement the program's operations.

Register Allocation: Efficiently allocating registers to variables to minimize memory access.

Instruction Scheduling: Reordering instructions to maximize instruction-level parallelism.

Memory Access Optimization: Optimizing memory access patterns to reduce cache misses and improve performance.

By understanding the target machine architecture, compilers can generate highly optimized code that takes full advantage of the hardware's capabilities. This can lead to significant performance improvements in the generated programs.

7.2 Instruction Selection and Code Emission

Instruction selection and code emission are the final stages of the compilation process. They involve translating the intermediate representation (IR) into machine code for the target architecture.

Instruction Selection

Instruction selection is the process of choosing the appropriate machine instructions from the target machine's instruction set to implement the operations specified in the IR. The goal is to select instructions that are efficient and accurate.

Key considerations for instruction selection:

Instruction set architecture: The available instructions and their properties.

Operand types: The types of operands used in the IR (e.g., integer, floating-point, pointer).

Operator mapping: Mapping high-level operations (e.g., addition, multiplication) to low-level machine instructions.

Cost model: Estimating the cost of different instruction sequences to select the most efficient one.

Code Emission

Code emission is the process of generating the actual machine code instructions. It involves:

Instruction encoding: Encoding the selected instructions into binary format.

Register allocation: Assigning registers to variables and temporary values.

Memory management: Generating code to access memory, including load and store instructions.

Control flow generation: Generating code for control flow constructs like jumps, branches, and loops.

Challenges in Instruction Selection and Code Emission:

Complex instruction sets: Modern processors often have complex instruction sets with many variations and special-purpose instructions.

Multiple instruction sequences: There may be multiple ways to implement a particular operation, and the compiler must choose the most efficient one.

Resource constraints: The number of available registers and the capacity of the instruction cache can limit the optimization opportunities.

By effectively performing instruction selection and code emission, compilers can generate highly efficient machine code that maximizes the performance of the target hardware.

7.3 Code Optimization for Specific Architectures

Code optimization for specific architectures involves tailoring the generated code to the unique characteristics of the target hardware. This can significantly improve performance and efficiency. Here are some key techniques:

1. Exploiting Instruction Set Architecture (ISA) Features:

SIMD Instructions: Utilizing Single Instruction, Multiple Data (SIMD) instructions to perform parallel operations on multiple data elements.

Vectorization: Identifying and vectorizing loops to take advantage of SIMD instructions.

Special-Purpose Instructions: Leveraging specialized instructions for specific operations (e.g., floating-point, cryptography).

2. Memory Hierarchy Optimization:

Cache-Friendly Code: Arranging data access patterns to maximize cache hit rates.

Loop Tiling: Breaking large loops into smaller tiles to improve cache locality.

Prefetching: Predicting future memory accesses and prefetching data into the cache.

3. Pipeline Optimization:

Instruction Scheduling: Reordering instructions to maximize instruction-level parallelism and minimize pipeline stalls.

Branch Prediction: Predicting the outcome of branches to avoid pipeline stalls.

4. Processor-Specific Optimizations:

Out-of-Order Execution: Taking advantage of out-of-order execution capabilities to hide latency.

Superscalar Execution: Exploiting multiple execution units to execute multiple instructions in parallel.

Hardware-Specific Optimizations: Using specific hardware features, such as hardware loop unrolling or prefetching units.

5. Compiler Flags and Options:

Optimization Levels: Selecting appropriate optimization levels to balance performance and code size.

Target-Specific Flags: Using flags to specify the target architecture and its specific features.

Profiling and Feedback-Directed Optimization: Analyzing the performance of the generated code and making further optimizations based on the results.

Example: For a modern x86 processor, a compiler might optimize code by:

Vectorizing loops: Using SIMD instructions to process multiple elements in a single instruction.

Loop unrolling: Reducing loop overhead by unrolling the loop and replicating the loop body.

Instruction scheduling: Reordering instructions to maximize instruction-level parallelism.

Cache-friendly memory access: Arranging data access patterns to improve cache locality.

By carefully considering the target architecture and applying appropriate optimization techniques, compilers can generate highly efficient and optimized code.

Chapter 8

Runtime Environment

8.1 Memory Management: Stack, Heap, and Garbage Collection

Memory management is a critical aspect of programming language implementation, ensuring efficient allocation and deallocation of memory resources. Three primary memory allocation strategies are commonly used: stack, heap, and garbage collection.

Stack Memory

Characteristics:

LIFO (Last-In-First-Out) structure.

Automatic memory allocation and deallocation.

Used for function calls, local variables, and return addresses.

Advantages:

Fast allocation and deallocation.

Simple to manage.

Disadvantages:

Fixed size.

Potential for stack overflow if too many function calls are nested.

Heap Memory

Characteristics:

Dynamic memory allocation.

Used for objects and data structures that need to persist beyond function calls.

Requires explicit memory management (e.g., manual allocation and deallocation).

Advantages:

Flexible size.

Can accommodate large data structures.

Disadvantages:

Slower allocation and deallocation.

Risk of memory leaks if memory is not deallocated properly.

Garbage Collection

Characteristics:

Automatic memory management.

The garbage collector identifies and reclaims unused memory.

Used in many modern languages (e.g., Java, Python, JavaScript).

Advantages:

Reduces the risk of memory leaks.

Simplifies memory management for programmers.

Disadvantages:

Can introduce performance overhead.

Can cause unpredictable pauses during garbage collection.

Common Garbage Collection Algorithms:

Mark-and-Sweep: Marks reachable objects and sweeps unmarked objects for reclamation.

Reference Counting: Tracks the number of references to an object and reclaims objects with zero references.

Generational Garbage Collection: Divides memory into generations and applies different garbage collection strategies to each generation.

Choosing the Right Memory Management Strategy: The choice of memory management strategy depends on various factors, including:

Language paradigm: Procedural languages often rely on stack-based memory allocation, while object-oriented languages typically use heap-based allocation.

Performance requirements: Real-time systems may require deterministic memory allocation and deallocation, while general-purpose applications may prioritize flexibility and convenience.

Memory usage: The amount of memory required by the application will influence the choice of strategy.

By understanding these memory management techniques, programmers can write more efficient and reliable code.

8.2 Exception Handling

Exception handling is a mechanism in programming languages that allows for the detection, interception, and handling of runtime errors or exceptional conditions. It helps to prevent program crashes and provides a way to gracefully recover from errors.

Key Concepts:

Exception: An event that occurs during program execution that disrupts the normal flow of control.

Try Block: A block of code where exceptions might occur.

Catch Block: A block of code that handles specific types of exceptions.

Finally Block: A block of code that is always executed, regardless of whether an exception is thrown or not.

Throw: A statement that raises an exception.

Basic Exception Handling Structure:

```
try {
    // Code that might throw an exception
} catch (ExceptionType1 exceptionObject1) {
    // Handle ExceptionType1
} catch (ExceptionType2 exceptionObject2) {
    // Handle ExceptionType2
} finally {
    // Code that always executes
}
```

Example (Python):

Python

```
try:
    x = int(input("Enter a number: "))
    y = 10 / x
except ZeroDivisionError:
    print("Error: Division by zero")
except ValueError:
    print("Error: Invalid input")
```

```
else:
    print("Result:", y)
finally:
    print("Execution complete")
```

Benefits of Exception Handling:

Robustness: Prevents program crashes by handling errors gracefully.

Error Isolation: Isolates error handling code from the main program flow.

Code Readability: Improves code readability by separating error handling from normal execution.

Custom Error Handling: Allows for custom error handling based on specific exception types.

Best Practices for Exception Handling:

Use exceptions for exceptional conditions: Avoid using exceptions for normal control flow.

Provide informative error messages: Include relevant information about the error in the exception message.

Handle exceptions at the appropriate level: Handle exceptions at the highest level where you can provide the best solution.

Avoid excessive use of try-catch blocks: Use them judiciously to avoid cluttering the code.

Clean up resources in the finally block: Ensure that resources like file handles and network connections are released properly.

By effectively using exception handling, you can write more reliable and robust programs.

8.3 Input/Output Operations

Input/Output (I/O) operations are essential for any program to interact with external devices, such as keyboards, monitors, files, and networks. These operations allow programs to receive input data and produce output results.

Types of I/O Operations

Standard Input/Output:

Standard Input (stdin): Typically the keyboard.

Standard Output (stdout): Typically the console or terminal.

Standard Error (stderr): Used for error messages and debugging output.

File I/O:

Reading and writing data to files on disk.

Operations include opening, closing, reading, writing, and appending files.

Network I/O:

Communicating with other computers over a network.

Involves sending and receiving data over network protocols like TCP/IP.

I/O Operations in Programming Languages
C/C++:

Standard I/O: `printf`, `scanf`, `fprintf`, `fscanf`.

File I/O: `fopen`, `fclose`, `fread`, `fwrite`, `fgets`, `fputs`.

Network I/O: `socket`, `connect`, `bind`, `listen`, `send`, `recv`.

Python:

Standard I/O: `print`, `input`.

File I/O: `open`, `read`, `write`, `close`.

Network I/O: `socket` module.

Java:

Standard I/O: `System.out.println`, `Scanner`.

File I/O: `FileReader`, `FileWriter`, `BufferedReader`, `BufferedWriter`.

Network I/O: `Socket`, `ServerSocket`.

Key Considerations for I/O Operations

Efficiency: Optimize I/O operations to minimize overhead and improve performance.

Error Handling: Implement robust error handling to handle potential exceptions and failures.

Security: Protect against security vulnerabilities, especially when dealing with network I/O.

Asynchronous I/O: Utilize asynchronous I/O techniques to improve concurrency and responsiveness.

Buffering: Use buffering to improve performance by reducing the number of system calls.

By understanding the different types of I/O operations and their implementation in programming languages, you can write efficient and reliable programs that interact with the outside world.

Chapter 9

Interpreters

9.1 Virtual Machines and Bytecode

A virtual machine (VM) is a software implementation of a computer system that executes programs independently of the underlying hardware. It provides an abstraction layer that allows programs to run on different hardware platforms without modification.

Bytecode is a low-level representation of machine code that is specific to a particular virtual machine. It is typically generated by a compiler and interpreted or just-in-time (JIT) compiled by the virtual machine.

Why Use Virtual Machines and Bytecode?

Platform Independence: Programs compiled to bytecode can run on any platform with a compatible virtual machine.

Security: Virtual machines can isolate programs from the host system, reducing the risk of security breaches.

Portability: Bytecode can be easily distributed and executed on different systems.

Sandboxing: Virtual machines can be used to create sandboxed environments for running untrusted code.

Performance Optimization: Just-in-time compilation can significantly improve the performance of bytecode-based programs.

Common Virtual Machines and Bytecode Formats

Java Virtual Machine (JVM): Executes Java bytecode.

.NET Common Language Runtime (CLR): Executes Common Intermediate Language (CIL) bytecode.

Python Virtual Machine (PVM): Executes Python bytecode.

WebAssembly (WASM): A binary format for web applications that can be executed in web browsers.

How Virtual Machines Work

1 Bytecode Loading: The virtual machine loads the bytecode into memory.

2 Bytecode Interpretation: The virtual machine interprets the bytecode instructions one by one and executes the corresponding operations.

3 Just-In-Time (JIT) Compilation: The virtual machine can dynamically compile frequently executed bytecode into native machine code, improving performance.

4 Memory Management: The virtual machine manages memory allocation and deallocation for the program.

5 Security: The virtual machine can restrict the program's access to system resources to enhance security.

By using virtual machines and bytecode, developers can create portable, secure, and efficient software applications that can run on a wide range of hardware platforms.

9.2 Interpreter Design and Implementation

An interpreter is a computer program that directly executes instructions written in a programming language. It analyzes the source code line by line, translates it into machine code, and executes it immediately.

Key Components of an Interpreter

1 Lexer:

Breaks the source code into tokens (keywords, identifiers, operators, literals).

Ignores whitespace and comments.

2 Parser:

Analyzes the token stream to construct a parse tree or abstract syntax tree (AST).

Checks the syntax of the code.

3 Semantic Analyzer:

Checks the semantic correctness of the code.

Performs type checking and scope resolution.

4 Interpreter Engine:

Executes the code represented by the AST.

Manages the program's execution environment.

Handles memory allocation and deallocation.

Implementation Techniques

1. Recursive Descent Parsing:

A top-down parsing technique where each non-terminal symbol in the grammar is represented by a recursive function.

Simple to implement but can be inefficient for complex grammars.

2. Table-Driven Parsing:

Uses a parsing table to guide the parsing process.

More efficient than recursive descent parsing, especially for complex grammars.

3. Interpretive Execution:

Directly interprets the AST or bytecode generated by the parser.

Slower than compiled code but offers flexibility.

4. Just-In-Time (JIT) Compilation:

Dynamically compiles frequently executed code into machine code.

Improves performance significantly compared to pure interpretation.

Challenges in Interpreter Design and Implementation

Performance: Interpreters are generally slower than compiled programs.

Memory Usage: Interpreters often require more memory than compiled programs.

Complexity: Implementing a full-featured interpreter can be complex.

Error Handling: Interpreters need to handle various types of errors, including syntax errors, semantic errors, and runtime errors.

In conclusion, interpreters play a vital role in programming language implementation, offering flexibility and rapid development. By understanding the key components and implementation techniques, you can build efficient and robust interpreters for various programming languages.

9.3 Just-In-Time Compilation

Just-In-Time (JIT) compilation is a technique used to improve the performance of interpreted programs. It involves compiling bytecode into native machine code during program execution, rather than before execution. This allows for dynamic optimization based on runtime information.

How JIT Compilation Works:

1 Bytecode Loading: The program's bytecode is loaded into memory.

2 Profiling: The virtual machine profiles the running program to identify frequently executed code sections, or "hot spots."

3 Compilation: The JIT compiler compiles the identified hot spots into native machine code.

4 Execution: The compiled native code is executed directly, which is significantly faster than interpreting bytecode.

Advantages of JIT Compilation:

Improved Performance: JIT compilation can significantly boost the performance of interpreted languages by converting them to efficient machine code.

Dynamic Optimization: JIT compilers can adapt to the specific hardware and software environment, making optimizations tailored to the system.

Flexibility: JIT compilation allows for dynamic code generation and optimization, which can be useful for certain applications.

Disadvantages of JIT Compilation:

Startup Time: The initial startup time of a JIT-compiled program can be longer due to the compilation overhead.

Memory Overhead: JIT compilation requires additional memory for storing compiled code.

Complexity: Implementing a high-performance JIT compiler is a complex task.

Examples of Languages Using JIT Compilation:

Java: The Java Virtual Machine (JVM) uses a JIT compiler to improve the performance of Java applications.

Python: Some Python implementations, such as PyPy, use JIT compilation to accelerate Python code.

JavaScript: Modern JavaScript engines like V8 (used in Chrome and Node.js) employ JIT compilation to optimize JavaScript code.

By combining the flexibility of interpretation with the performance of compiled code, JIT compilation has become a powerful technique for improving the performance of many programming languages.

Chapter 10

Advanced Topics

10.1 Domain-Specific Languages (DSLs)

A Domain-Specific Language (DSL) is a computer language tailored to a specific problem domain. Unlike general-purpose languages like Python or Java, which are designed to solve a wide range of problems, DSLs are optimized for a particular task or set of tasks.

Why Use DSLs?

Increased Productivity: DSLs can significantly improve productivity by allowing domain experts to express solutions in a more concise and intuitive way.

Reduced Complexity: DSLs can simplify complex tasks by abstracting away unnecessary details and providing a higher level of abstraction.

Improved Quality: DSLs can help to ensure code quality by enforcing domain-specific constraints and best practices.

Better Communication: DSLs can facilitate communication between domain experts and software developers by providing a shared language.

Types of DSLs:

1 Internal DSLs:

Embedded within a general-purpose language.

Often achieved through syntactic sugar or metaprogramming techniques.

Examples: Ruby on Rails configuration files, SQL embedded in Java.

2 External DSLs:

Standalone languages with their own syntax and semantics.

Require a separate parser and interpreter or compiler.

Examples: HTML, CSS, regular expressions.

Examples of DSLs:

SQL: A language for querying and manipulating databases.

Regular Expressions: A language for pattern matching in text.

HTML/CSS: Languages for structuring and styling web pages.

Makefile: A language for specifying build processes.

Verilog/VHDL: Languages for designing hardware circuits.

Creating DSLs:

1 Define the Domain: Clearly identify the problem domain and its specific requirements.

2 Design the Syntax: Create a simple and intuitive syntax that aligns with the domain concepts.

3 Implement the Parser: Develop a parser to analyze the DSL code and generate an abstract syntax tree (AST).

4 Implement the Semantics: Define the meaning of the DSL constructs and how they are executed.

5 Integrate with a Host Language: If necessary, integrate the DSL with a general-purpose language to provide additional functionality.

By carefully designing and implementing DSLs, developers can significantly improve the productivity and quality of software development in specific domains.

10.2 Compiler Construction Tools

Compiler construction tools are software applications that aid in the development of compilers. These tools automate many of the tedious and error-prone tasks involved in compiler development, such as lexical analysis, parsing, semantic analysis, code generation, and optimization.

Popular Compiler Construction Tools:

1 Lex:

A lexical analyzer generator that automatically generates lexical analyzers from regular expressions.

Creates tokenizers that recognize patterns in the input stream.

2 Yacc (Yet Another Compiler-Compiler):

A parser generator that automatically generates parsers from context-free grammars.

Creates parsers that analyze the syntactic structure of the input.

2 ANTLR (ANother Tool for Language Recognition):

A powerful parser generator that can generate parsers for a wide range of grammars, including context-sensitive grammars.

Offers features like tree grammars, actions, and embedded languages.

3 LLVM (Low Level Virtual Machine):

A modular compiler infrastructure that provides a variety of tools and libraries for compiler development.

Includes a compiler front-end, optimizer, and code generator.

4 GCC (GNU Compiler Collection):

A versatile compiler suite that supports multiple programming languages, including C, C++, and Fortran.

Can be used as a reference implementation for learning compiler design.

Key Features of Compiler Construction Tools:

Automation of routine tasks: These tools automate the generation of lexical analyzers and parsers, saving time and effort.

Error detection and reporting: They help identify and report errors in the input code.

Code generation: They can generate efficient machine code for different target architectures.

Optimization: They support various optimization techniques to improve the performance of generated code.

Debugging facilities: They provide tools for debugging and analyzing the compiler's behavior.

By using these tools, compiler developers can focus on the core aspects of compiler design, such as language semantics, optimization techniques, and code generation strategies. These tools significantly accelerate the development process and improve the quality of the generated compilers.

10.3 Parallel and Distributed Compilation

Parallel and distributed compilation techniques aim to speed up the compilation process by dividing the workload across multiple processors or machines. This can significantly reduce compilation time, especially for large projects.

Parallel Compilation

Parallel compilation involves dividing the compilation process into smaller tasks that can be executed concurrently on multiple cores of a single machine.

Common Techniques:

1 Task-Level Parallelism:

Divide the compilation process into independent tasks, such as lexical analysis, parsing, semantic analysis, and code generation.

Assign these tasks to different cores.

2 Data-Level Parallelism:

Exploit parallelism within individual compilation phases, such as parallel parsing or code generation for different parts of the program.

Distributed Compilation

Distributed compilation extends the concept of parallel compilation to multiple machines. It involves partitioning the compilation workload across a network of computers.

Common Techniques:

1 Remote Compilation:

Offload compilation tasks to remote machines, especially for resource-intensive tasks like optimization and code generation.

2 Distributed Build Systems:

Use distributed build systems like `Distcc` or `SCons` to coordinate compilation across multiple machines.

3 Distributed Code Generation:

Divide the code generation process into smaller tasks and distribute them to different machines.

Challenges and Considerations

Communication Overhead: Coordinating and synchronizing tasks across multiple machines can introduce communication overhead.

Load Balancing: Distributing the workload evenly among machines is crucial for optimal performance.

Data Dependency: Some compilation tasks may depend on the results of previous tasks, limiting the degree of parallelism.

Tool and Infrastructure Requirements: Distributed compilation requires a suitable network infrastructure and compatible compiler tools.

Benefits of Parallel and Distributed Compilation

Reduced Compilation Time: By leveraging multiple processors or machines, compilation time can be significantly reduced.

Improved Scalability: Distributed compilation can handle large projects with many source files.

Enhanced Resource Utilization: By distributing the workload, idle computing resources can be utilized effectively.

By effectively applying parallel and distributed compilation techniques, developers can accelerate the software development process and improve productivity.

www.ingramcontent.com/pod-product-compliance
Lightning Source LLC
Chambersburg PA
CBHW070411230526
45471CB00006B/2754